Gone Forever!
Velociraptor

Rupert Matthews

Heinemann
LIBRARY

www.heinemann.co.uk/library

Visit our website to find out more information about Heinemann Library books.

To order:

 Phone ++44 (0)1865 888066

Send a fax to ++44 (0)1865 314091

Visit the Heinemann Bookshop at www.heinemann.co.uk/library to browse our catalogue and order online.

First published in Great Britain by Heinemann Library, Halley Court, Jordan Hill, Oxford OX2 8EJ, a part of Harcourt Education. Heinemann is a registered trademark of Harcourt Education Ltd.

© Harcourt Education Ltd 2003.
First published in paperback in 2004.
The moral right of the proprietor has been asserted.

Editorial: Andrew Farrow and Dan Nunn
Design: Ron Kamen and Paul Davies and Associates
Illustrations: James Field of Simon Girling and Associates
Picture Research: Rebecca Sodergren and Ginny Stroud-Lewis
Production: Viv Hichens
Originated by Ambassador Litho Ltd
Printed and bound in China by South China Printing Company

07 06 05 04 03
10 9 8 7 6 5 4 3 2 1
ISBN 0 431 16615 3
(hardback)

08 07 06 05 04
10 9 8 7 6 5 4 3 2 1
ISBN 0 431 16620 X
(paperback)

British Library Cataloguing in Publication Data

Matthews, Rupert
Velociraptor. - (Gone forever)
1. Velociraptor - Juvenile literature
I. Title
567.9'12

Acknowledgements

The Publishers are grateful to the following for permission to reproduce copyright material: American Museum of Natural History pp. 12, 18, 20, 22, 24; Corbis pp. 6 (Robert Campbell/Sygma), 10 (Layne Kennedy); Geoscience Features pp. 8, 14; Natural History Museum, London pp. 4, 26; Oregon State University p. 16.

Cover photo reproduced with permission of the American Museum of Natural History.

Our thanks to Dr Angela Milner of the Natural History Museum, London for her assistance in the preparation of this book.

Every effort has been made to contact copyright holders of any material reproduced in this book. Any omissions will be rectified in subsequent printings if notice is given to the Publishers.

Disclaimer

Contents

Some words are shown in bold, **like this**.
You can find out what they mean by looking in the Glossary.

Gone forever!

Some animals are **extinct**. This means that they have all died and none are left alive. **Fossils** of these animals are studied by scientists called **palaeontologists**. They find out about the animal and how it lived.

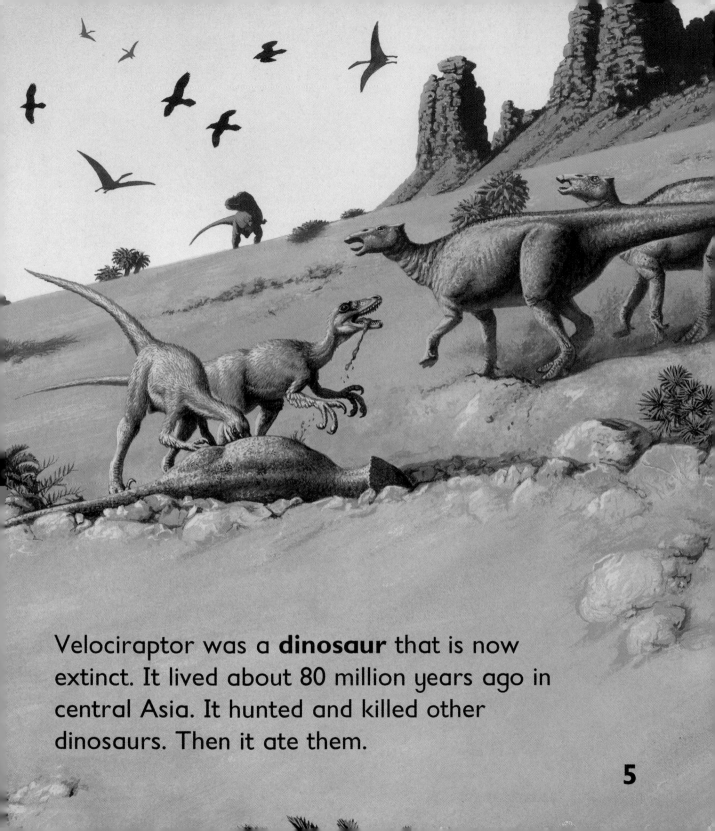

Velociraptor was a **dinosaur** that is now
extinct. It lived about 80 million years ago in
central Asia. It hunted and killed other
dinosaurs. Then it ate them.

Velociraptor's hunting grounds

Scientists called **geologists** study the rocks where **fossils** are found. The geologists can learn about the places where **dinosaurs** lived by looking at the rocks.

Velociraptor lived in places that were fairly dry and warm. There were some trees. Most of the land was covered by desert, but there were some scrubby bushes and other short plants.

The flowers

Scientists have found **fossils** of plants in the same rocks as Velociraptor fossils. These show what sorts of plants grew in the land of Velociraptor. A few of these plants may have had bright, colourful flowers.

fossil of a plant

Some of the plants at the time of Velociraptor were flowering bushes. In some places, these were like the modern plant called **magnolia**. Others plants were different from plants that grow today. As well as bushes, there were also a few fir and pine trees.

9

Living with Velociraptor

Many other types of animal lived alongside Velociraptor. Some of these were birds. Not many bird **fossils** from the time of Velociraptor have survived. This fossil of a feather is from many million years later.

Birds probably lived among the bushes. Some would eat the new types of **insects** that lived at this time. These included butterflies and bees, which fed on the flowers. Flying **reptiles** called **pterosaurs** glided higher in the skies.

What was Velociraptor?

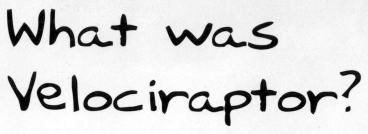

Palaeontologists have studied the **fossils** of Velociraptor. They used the fossils to find out what kind of animal Velociraptor was. The teeth show the sort of food Velociraptor ate. The **limbs** show how it obtained that food.

12

Velociraptor was a hunter, or **predator**. It killed and ate other **dinosaurs**. It was about two metres long. It had sharp claws and teeth. It used these to attack other dinosaurs.

13

Velociraptor nests

Scientists have found **fossils** of **dinosaur** eggs like the ones below. This nest belonged to a dinosaur called Oviraptor. The eggs were laid in a circle with the narrow end down in the nest. Scientists think that Velociraptor laid its eggs in a similar way.

Oviraptor eggs

The mother Velociraptor probably stayed near
the nest. She would protect the eggs from any
animals that tried to eat them. The mother made
sure the eggs stayed warm. She might even have
sat on the nest.

15

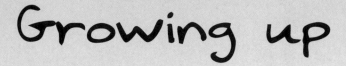

Growing up

Fossils of young hunting **dinosaurs** have been found. These show that baby Velociraptor may have hunted from the day it **hatched**. However, it was not as strong as an adult. Its claws had not yet grown to full size.

fossil of a baby Scipionyx dinosaur

Baby Velociraptor was too small to hunt other dinosaurs. It probably fed on **lizards** and other small animals. It may even have hunted **insects**, such as beetles. As it grew older the Velociraptor began to kill larger animals.

17

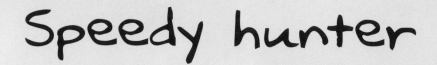

Speedy hunter

Velociraptor had strong back legs and a long, stiff tail. **Fossils** show that these were connected to very powerful **muscles** over the hips. This meant that Velociraptor could run quickly, and change direction suddenly.

This fossil is Deinonychus, a dinosaur like Velociraptor.

Scientists believe that Velociraptor hunted its **prey** by dashing between bushes and shrubs. Its long legs and light weight meant it was very fast. The name Velociraptor means 'fast hunter'. Scientists also think that Velociraptor hunted in **packs**.

Killer claws!

The back feet of Velociraptor were very unusual. The second toe of each foot had a huge, curved claw.

The claw was very sharp. The toe could be flicked forwards with great force. This stabbed into Velociraptor's **prey**.

Scientists think the claws of Velociraptor were like Deinonychus, shown here.

Scientists think that Velociraptor hunted other
dinosaurs. It attacked them with its large claw.
It may have leapt at a victim and killed it with
one mighty kick! Here, a Velociraptor is attacking
a Protoceratops.

Night fighter

The **fossil** skull of Velociraptor shows it had large eyes. Other creatures with large eyes can see well in dim light. Scientists think Velociraptor may have been able to see well at night.

Velociraptor skull

Velociraptor may have hunted by moonlight or in the poor light of dusk. Other **dinosaurs** would have tried to hide in the shadows. They hoped that the hunter would not see them.

Food for Velociraptor

One **fossil** of Velociraptor has been found with its claws wrapped around the **frill** of a dinosaur called Protoceratops. Protoceratops ate plants. Scientists believe that Protoceratops was a favourite **prey** of Velociraptor.

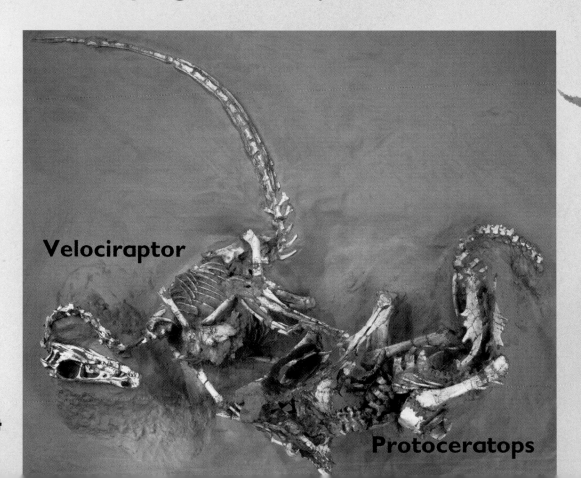

Velociraptor

Protoceratops

24

Protoceratops walked on all four legs. It could
hide from Velociraptor among the bushes.
Protoceratops had a powerful **beak** for eating
tough plants. It could use the beak to bite at
Velociraptor.

25

The feathered killer

Scientists have found some very well preserved **fossils** of small hunting **dinosaurs**. The dinosaurs were covered with feathers. These fossils show that birds are related to dinosaurs.

feathers

Most scientists think that Velociraptor had
feathers, too. It may have had short feathers on its
body to keep it warm, with longer feathers on its
tail and arms. These may have been very colourful.

Velociraptor around the world

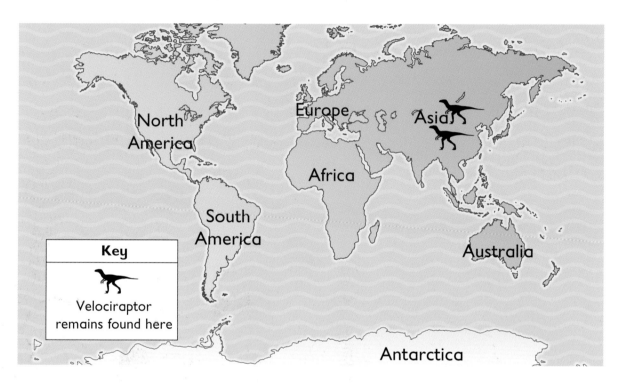

Key

Velociraptor remains found here

The **fossils** of Velociraptor have been found in Asia. They were discovered in the Gobi Desert, which covers parts of China and Mongolia.

When did Velociraptor live?

Velociraptor lived on Earth in the Age of the **Dinosaurs**. Scientists call this the Mesozoic Era. Velociraptor lived between 80 and 77 million years ago (mya). This was near the end of what scientists call the Cretaceous Period.

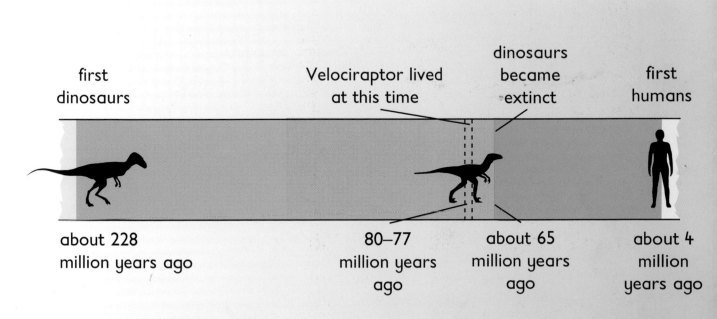

first dinosaurs

Velociraptor lived at this time

dinosaurs became extinct

first humans

about 228 million years ago

80–77 million years ago

about 65 million years ago

about 4 million years ago

Fact file

Velociraptor fact file	
Length:	up to 2 metres
Height:	up to 1.5 metres
Weight:	about 15 kilograms
Time:	Late Cretaceous Period, about 80 million years ago
Place:	Central Asia

How to say it

Velociraptor – vee-loss-ee-rapp-torr
Cretaceaus – kri-tay-shus
dinosaur – dine-oh-saw
palaeontologist – pal-ee-on-tol-o-jist
Protoceratops – proe-toe-serr-ah-topps
pterosaur – terr-uh-saw

Glossary

beak sharp layer of horn used in place of teeth

dinosaurs reptiles that lived on Earth between 228 and 65 million years ago. Dinosaurs are extinct.

extinct an animal is extinct when there are none left alive

fossils remains of a plant or animal, usually found in rocks

frill a fringe of bone at the back of some dinosaurs' head. Protoceratops and Triceratops had frills.

geologist a scientist who studies rocks is called a geologist

hatch break out of an egg

insect small creature with six legs

limb an arm or a leg

lizard a type of reptile that usually has a big body and tail, four legs and eyelids that move

magnolia a bush with woody branches and dark green leaves. It has white flowers.

muscles parts of an animal's body that provide power to make it move

pack a group of animals that lives and hunts together

palaeontologist scientist who studies fossils to discover about extinct animals, such as dinosaurs

predator animal which hunts other animals for food

prey an animal that is hunted and eaten by another animal is known as its prey

pterosaurs flying reptiles that lived at the same time as the dinosaurs. They looked similar to modern bats but were not related. There were several different types of pterosaur.

reptile animal with scaly skin. Snakes, lizards and crocodiles are all reptiles.

Find out more

These are some other books about dinosaurs:

Velociraptor, Elaina Landau (Children's Press, 1999)
Big Book of Dinosaurs, Angela Wilkes (Dorling Kindersley, 1994)
Dinosaur Park, Nick Denchfield (Macmillan, 1998)

Look on these websites for more information:

www.bbc.co.uk/dinosaurs/fact_files/
www.enchantedlearning.com/subjects/dinos/
www.oink.demon.co.uk/topics/dinosaur.htm

Index